TOUCHDOWN NOUNS

By Doris Fisher and D. L. Gibbs
Illustrated by Scott Angle
Curriculum consultant: Candia Bowles, M.Ed., M.S.

Gareth Stevens
Publishing

Please visit our web site at **www.garethstevens.com**.
For a free color catalog describing Gareth Stevens Publishing's list of high-quality books, call 1-800-542-2595 (USA) or 1-800-387-3178 (Canada). Gareth Stevens Publishing's fax: 1-877-542-2596

Library of Congress Cataloging-in-Publication Data

Fisher, Doris.
    Grammar all-stars / Doris Fisher and D. L. Gibbs.
       p. cm.
    ISBN-10: 0-8368-8906-1   ISBN-13: 978-0-8368-8906-2 (lib. bdg.)
    ISBN-10: 0-8368-8913-4   ISBN-13: 978-0-8368-8913-0 (pbk.)
   1. English language—Grammar—Juvenile literature. 2. English language—Parts of speech—Juvenile literature. 3. Sports—Juvenile literature. I. Gibbs, D.L. II. Title.
   PE1112.F538   2008
   428.2—dc22   2007033840

This edition first published in 2008 by
Gareth Stevens Publishing
A Weekly Reader® Company
1 Reader's Digest Road
Pleasantville, NY 10570-7000 USA

Senior Managing Editor: Lisa M. Guidone
Senior Editor: Barbara Bakowski
Creative Director: Lisa Donovan
Senior Designer: Keith Plechaty

Printed in the United States of America

1 2 3 4 5 6 7 8 9 10 09 08 07

CONTENTS

CHAPTER 1

THE NAME OF THE GAME

What Are Proper and Common Nouns?................................ **4**

CHAPTER 2

THE PLAYERS

Singular and Plural Nouns.. **12**

CHAPTER 3

KICK, PASS, TOUCHDOWN!

Signals and Possession.. **20**

BUZZ STAR PLAYS BY THE RULES!..........**30**

ALL-STAR ACTIVITY................................**31**

Look for the **boldface** words on each page.
Then read the **TOUCHDOWN TIP** that follows.

CHAPTER 1

THE NAME OF THE GAME

What Are Proper and Common Nouns?

"Hurry up, **Lizzie**!" says **announcer Buzz Star** of **P-L-A-Y TV**. "I can't be late for the **Blue Ribbon Bowl**."

"I'm coming, **Uncle Buzz**," says **Lizzie**. "I was trying to finish my **homework**. **Nouns** are confusing! There are so many different **kinds**."

"**Nouns** are easy, **Lizzie**," says **Buzz**. "They are **words** that name **things**. Right now the only **noun** I can think about is **game**. It's getting late. Let's go!"

"I hope I don't throw any **gutter balls**," says **Lizzie**. "I want to knock down all the **pins** and score a **strike**!"

"No, **Lizzie**," says **Buzz**. "We're not bowling! We're going to watch **football**! And it's not just any **game**. The **Blue Ribbon Bowl** is special. It's the most important **game** of the **year**."

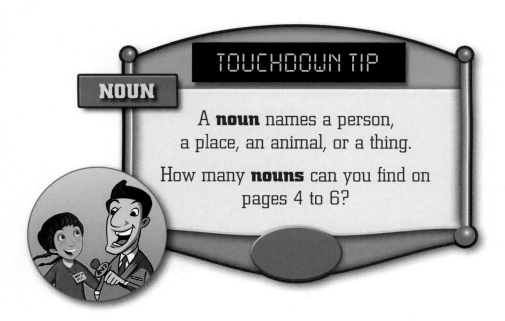

TOUCHDOWN TIP

NOUN

A **noun** names a person, a place, an animal, or a thing.

How many **nouns** can you find on pages 4 to 6?

7

"Hmmm," says **Lizzie**. "That means **Blue Ribbon Bowl** is a proper noun. Right, **Uncle Buzz**?"

"That's right, **Lizzie**," says **Buzz**. "**Sky High Stadium** is a proper noun, too. That's the name of the particular football stadium we're going to. The **Rockets** are playing the **Tigers**. Those names are also proper nouns."

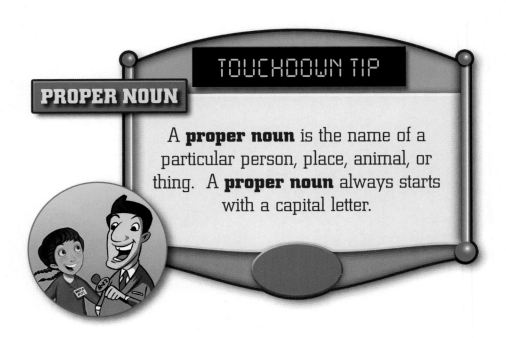

TOUCHDOWN TIP

PROPER NOUN

A **proper noun** is the name of a particular person, place, animal, or thing. A **proper noun** always starts with a capital letter.

"Wait a **minute**," says Lizzie. "I thought **rocket** and **tiger** were common **nouns**."

"The kind of **rocket** you fly and a **tiger** at the **zoo** are common **nouns**," says Buzz. "The Rockets and the Tigers I'm talking about are special **names** for **teams**. Each **name** starts with a capital **letter**, just as yours does, Lizzie."

"I think I understand!" says Lizzie. "The word **tiger** is a common **noun** when it means a **kind** of **cat**. The **name** of my **cat** is Tiger. His **name** is a proper **noun**. It starts with a capital **letter**. The **tiger** at the **zoo** does not have a capital **letter**."

"Good **job**, Lizzie!" says Buzz. "You don't sound confused anymore."

"But I think my **cat** is," Lizzie says with a **laugh**. "Sometimes Tiger thinks he's a **tiger**."

TOUCHDOWN TIP

COMMON NOUN

A **common noun** is a word that names any kind of person, place, animal, or thing. A **common noun** does not start with a capital letter.

THE PLAYERS

Singular and Plural Nouns

"Hello, fans! Welcome to the **Blue Ribbon Bowl**. I'm your **announcer**, **Buzz Star**, reporting live for **P-L-A-Y TV**. My **niece**, **Lizzie**, is here with me in the **press box**. Tell the viewers about the **action** at **Sky High Stadium**, **Lizzie**."

"There are so many people here, **Uncle Buzz**," says **Lizzie**. "I've never seen such a big **crowd**. Look! Some players are running onto the **field**. Which **team** are they on, **Uncle Buzz**?"

A **singular noun** names one person, place, animal, or thing.

"Those **players** are the **Rockets**, Lizzie," says Buzz. "Here come the **Tigers**. Listen to the crowd cheer. Both **teams** have plenty of **fans** in the **stands**.

"When we arrived at the stadium today, Lizzie and I spent a few **minutes** talking to the two **quarterbacks**.

"Let's hear what they had to say," says Buzz. "Hit the red switch, Lizzie, to play the video for our **viewers**."

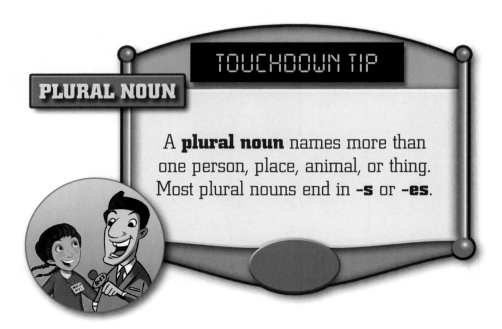

TOUCHDOWN TIP

PLURAL NOUN

A **plural noun** names more than one person, place, animal, or thing. Most plural nouns end in **-s** or **-es**.

"Buzz Star here, with my niece,
Lizzie. We're talking with John Turbo, the
quarterback for the Rockets. John, will the
fans see any surprise plays from your team
in the Blue Ribbon Bowl today?"

15

"Well, Buzz, we'll line up in the I formation. I'll be fast on my **feet**. My **men** on the line will be blocking for my runners."

"It sounds as if the Rockets will be soaring, John. Good luck out there.

"Now we're with Stan Stripes, the starting quarterback for the Tigers. Stan, you're the league leader in passing yards. What is your plan for the two **halves** of today's game?"

"Buzz, I'm going to grit my **teeth**, grab the ball, and fade back for the long bomb. My team will be blocking Rockets left and right."

TOUCHDOWN TIP

IRREGULAR PLURAL FORMS

Some singular nouns have **irregular plural forms**: foot = **feet**; man = **men**; half = **halves**; tooth = **teeth**.

"It sounds as if the Tigers will be roaring, Stan! We'll let you get back to the locker room.

"Don't change that channel, folks," says Buzz. "Lizzie and I will be back for the kickoff."

CHAPTER 3

KICK, PASS, TOUCHDOWN!

Signals and Possession

"Ladies and gentlemen, get ready for **the** toss," says Buzz. "Can you explain what's happening, Lizzie?"

"**An** official is flipping **a** coin," says Lizzie. "**The** quarterbacks are calling heads or tails."

"**The** Tigers won **the** toss, and they choose to kick," says Buzz. "Harry Katz boots **the** ball far. Joey Jett runs **the** ball back sixty yards for **the** Rockets! Wow, what **an** awesome run!"

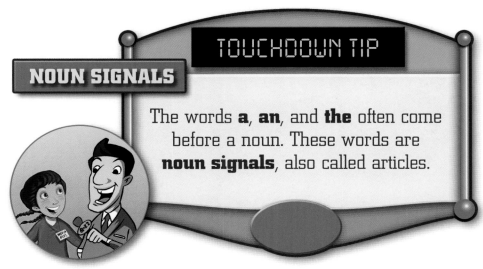

TOUCHDOWN TIP

NOUN SIGNALS

The words **a**, **an**, and **the** often come before a noun. These words are **noun signals**, also called articles.

"The **referee's** whistle is in his mouth," says Lizzie. "He is throwing something in the air."

"That is a penalty flag," says Buzz. "**Turbo's** shoe is untied! The referee is calling a penalty against the Rockets for delaying the game! The **coach's** face looks really angry."

TOUCHDOWN TIP

POSSESSIVE NOUNS

Singular nouns that end in **'s** are **possessive nouns**. **Possessive nouns** tell what or who owns something.

"I think the teams are ready to start playing again, Uncle Buzz!" says Lizzie.

"Turbo throws to Arrow Plane," says Buzz. "Plane catches the pass in the end zone!"

"TOUCHDOWN!" yells Lizzie.

"The **Rockets'** kicker, Max Power, makes the extra point," says Buzz. "The Rockets are on the scoreboard!

"Now it is the **Tigers'** ball," Buzz continues. "Rex Paws runs forty yards down the field. Harry Katz kicks a field goal for three points. The score is now Rockets 7, Tigers 3. The referee is making a time-out signal. It is the **Rockets'** time-out."

"Are those the **cheerleaders'** pom-poms near the **Rockets'** bench, Uncle Buzz?" asks Lizzie. "I hope I get to see the cheerleaders doing jumps and splits."

"The cheerleaders will perform during the halftime show," says Buzz. "A **children's** marching band is going to perform, too."

"How exciting!" says Lizzie. "I hope it is almost halftime!"

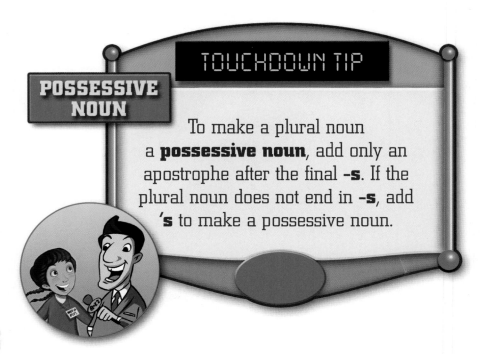

TOUCHDOWN TIP

POSSESSIVE NOUN

To make a plural noun a **possessive noun**, add only an apostrophe after the final **-s**. If the plural noun does not end in **-s**, add **'s** to make a possessive noun.

"… and the score at halftime is Rockets 14, Tigers 10," Buzz finally announces. "Each team scored one touchdown and kicked the extra point in the game's second quarter."

"Football games last a long time, Uncle Buzz," says Lizzie, late in the fourth quarter. "Why aren't the teams making touchdowns anymore?"

"The teams work hard to keep each other from scoring, Lizzie," says Buzz. "That's part of the game.

"After two scoreless quarters, with only thirty seconds left, it looks as if it's going to be a Rockets' victory," says Buzz. "This might be the last play of the game. Turbo fires the ball to Plane. Plane catches it and—oh, no! He fumbles. Paws picks up the ball for the Tigers and runs down the field. The Rockets can't catch him!"

"TOUCHDOWN!" yells Lizzie, jumping out of her seat.

"There's the final whistle," says Buzz. "The Tigers win the Blue Ribbon Bowl 16 to 14."

"Wow! That was fun, Uncle Buzz," says Lizzie.

"You couldn't ask for a more exciting ending," says Buzz. "Come on, Lizzie. Let's go get Sky High ice cream to celebrate!"

TOUCHDOWN TIP

How well do you know the rules? See how many nouns you can find on pages 27 to 29.

A **noun** is the name of a person, a place, an animal, or a thing.
Examples: teacher, Alaska, parrot, football

A **common noun** is the name of any person, place, animal, or thing.
Examples: man, stadium, dog, cereal

A **proper noun** names a specific, or particular, person, place, animal, or thing. A proper noun is always capitalized.
Examples: Buzz Star, Sky High Stadium, Rover, Quarterback Krispies

A **singular noun** names only one person, place, animal, or thing.
Examples: announcer, playground, cat, ball
A **plural noun** names more than one person, place, animal, or thing.
Examples: women, towns, foxes, strawberries

There are many ways to form **plural nouns**. For most nouns, add **-s** to a singular noun.
Example: quarterback/quarterbacks
Add **-es** to a singular noun that ends in **-s**, **-ch**, **-sh**, or **-x**.
Examples: glass/glasses, beach/beaches, dish/dishes, box/boxes
If the noun ends in **-y**, change the **y** to **i** and add **-es**.
Example: buddy/buddies

Some **plural nouns** do not follow the rules. They have **irregular forms**.
Plural nouns with irregular forms have to be memorized.
Examples: foot/feet   tooth/teeth   man/men

Possessive nouns tell what or who owns something.
Add **'s** to a **singular noun** to make it possessive.
Example: referee's whistle
Add **'s** to a **plural noun** that does <u>not</u> end in **-s**.
Example: children's book
Add only an apostrophe (') to a **plural noun** that ends in **-s**.
Example: dogs' bones

A, **an**, and **the** are **noun signals**.
A noun can come after each of these words in a sentence.
Examples: a touchdown, an announcer, the winners

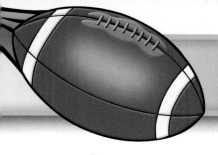

Lizzie wrote a thank-you letter to Uncle Buzz.
Can you find all the common and proper nouns?

Dear Uncle Buzz,

Thank you for taking me to the Blue Ribbon Bowl. It was fun to sit way up high in the press box. My friends could not believe I was on television!

Sky High Stadium is huge! I liked to watch the teams run up and down the field and score touchdowns. John Turbo and Stan Stripes are great quarterbacks. I also liked the noise from the crowd's cheers and the referees' whistles. The game was so exciting!

The cheerleaders did great flips and splits. I am a cheerleader at school. I hope I can perform in a show someday. Thanks again for a fun day and for the ice cream!

Your niece,
Lizzie

On a piece of paper, list all the **common nouns** in Lizzie's letter.
Then list all the **proper nouns**.

Label each noun on your list as
singular, **plural**, or **possessive**.

Turn the page to check your answers and to see how many points you scored!

31

ANSWER KEY

Did you find enough nouns to score a touchdown?

0–7 nouns: Fumble (oops!)   **15–21** nouns: Field Goal

8–14 nouns: First Down   **22–28** nouns: TOUCHDOWN!

COMMON NOUNS

1. press box
2. friends
3. television
4. teams
5. field
6. touchdowns
7. quarterbacks
8. noise
9. crowd's
10. cheers
11. referees'
12. whistles
13. game
14. cheerleaders
15. flips
16. splits
17. cheerleader
18. school
19. show
20. day
21. ice cream
22. niece

PROPER NOUNS

23. Uncle Buzz
24. Blue Ribbon Bowl
25. Sky High Stadium
26. John Turbo
27. Stan Stripes
28. Lizzie

All-Star Challenge

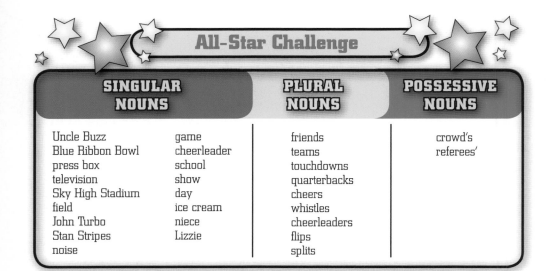

SINGULAR NOUNS		PLURAL NOUNS	POSSESSIVE NOUNS
Uncle Buzz	game	friends	crowd's
Blue Ribbon Bowl	cheerleader	teams	referees'
press box	school	touchdowns	
television	show	quarterbacks	
Sky High Stadium	day	cheers	
field	ice cream	whistles	
John Turbo	niece	cheerleaders	
Stan Stripes	Lizzie	flips	
noise		splits	